STRUNG
WOMEN
NEVER
GIVE
UP

Blue Mountain Arts®

New and Best-Selling Titles

By Susan Polis Schutz:

*To My Daughter with Love
on the Important Things in Life*

To My Grandchild with Love

To My Son with Love

～

By Douglas Pagels:

*Always Remember How Special
You Are to Me*

The Next Chapter of Your Life

Required Reading for All Teenagers

Simple Thoughts

You Are One Amazing Lady

～

By Minx Boren:

Healing Is a Journey

～

By Debra DiPietro:

Short Morning Prayers

By Marci:

Angels Are Everywhere!

Friends Are Forever

10 Simple Things to Remember

To My Daughter

To My Granddaughter

To My Mother

To My Sister

To My Son

You Are My "Once in a Lifetime"

～

By Carol Wiseman:

Emerging from the Heartache of Loss

～

By Latesha Randall:

The To-Be List

～

By Dr. Preston C. VanLoon:

The Path to Forgiveness

Anthologies:

A Daybook of Positive Thinking

Dream Big, Stay Positive, and Believe in Yourself

God Is Always Watching Over You

Life Isn't Always Easy …but It's Going to Be Okay

The Love Between a Mother and Daughter Is Forever

Nothing Fills the Heart with Joy like a Grandson

The Power of Prayer

A Son Is Life's Greatest Gift

Strong Women Never Give Up

There Is Nothing Sweeter in Life Than a Granddaughter

There Is So Much to Love About You… Daughter

Think Positive Thoughts Every Day

Words Every Teenager Should Remember

Words Every Woman Should Remember

STRONG WOMEN NEVER GIVE UP

Empowering Words for an Incredible Woman

Edited by Becky McKay

Blue Mountain Press™

Boulder, Colorado

Copyright © 2022 by Blue Mountain Arts, Inc.

All rights reserved. No part of this publication may be reproduced, stored in a retrieval system or transmitted in any form or by any means, electronic, mechanical, photocopying, recording or otherwise, without the written permission of the publisher.

We wish to thank Susan Polis Schutz for permission to reprint the following poems that appear in this publication: "If you know yourself well...," "So many choices...," "We who inherit the earth...," "Lean against a tree...," and "Sometimes you...." Copyright © 1982, 1986, 2001, 2017 by Stephen Schutz and Susan Polis Schutz. And for "Love is...." Copyright © 1977 by Continental Publications. Renewed © 2004 by Stephen Schutz and Susan Polis Schutz. All rights reserved.

Library of Congress Control Number: 2022937397
ISBN: 978-1-68088-384-8

and Blue Mountain Press are registered in U.S. Patent and Trademark Office.
Certain trademarks are used under license.

Acknowledgments appear on page 64.

Printed in China.
First Printing: 2022

This book is printed on recycled paper.

This book is printed on paper that has been specially produced to be acid free (neutral pH) and contains no groundwood or unbleached pulp. It conforms with the requirements of the American National Standards Institute, Inc., so as to ensure that this book will last and be enjoyed by future generations.

Blue Mountain Arts, Inc.
P.O. Box 4549, Boulder, Colorado 80306

Contents

(Authors listed in order of first appearance)

Strong Women Believe in Themselves

Believe in yourself.
Trust in your strengths.
Look in the mirror
and see what others see —
a talented, uplifting,
and magnificent woman
who can do anything
and everything she wants.

Believe in your heart
that you have the power
to grab hold of your future
and mold it into the things
you have always dreamed of.

Trust in your soul
that you are capable of doing
all that needs to be done.

Know that you are
incredible in every way
and see yourself
as others see you...
as an intelligent
and spectacular woman.

— Lamisha Serf-Walls

The way you see yourself
has a lasting impact on your life.
When you consider yourself
worthy of achieving your goals...
you'll become who you want to be.
You'll see yourself as confident and capable,
and you'll follow a different path —
because you now see yourself
    walking toward success.

We don't always realize
the full impact of our thoughts —
how far they reach
or how they truly affect us
    and our goals.
See yourself in this brand-new light.
Think you can — and you will.
Do all you can to become
everything you want to be.

— Barbara J. Hall

Strong Women
Know Their Own Worth

Take a moment to think about
how many people have smiled
   because of you —
about all the lives you've changed
   for the better,
sometimes without even trying.

Take a moment to look back
at all the joy you've caused
and all the good you've done,
even when you thought you were
   at your worst.

Take a moment to remember
how much love you've sent out there
and how much you matter to people,
just because you're you.

Now think about yourself for a moment
and remember that you deserve
all the best.

— Irina Vasilescu

We don't have to do anything to be glorious;
to be so is our nature. If we have read, studied,
and loved; if we have thought as deeply as
we could and felt as deeply as we could; if
our bodies are instruments of love given and
received — then we are the greatest blessing
in the world. Nothing needs to be added to
that to establish our worth.

— Marianne Williamson

And I will keep reminding myself,
every moment,
that I matter. That I am worthy.
That I am enough.
I will keep reminding myself
until the truth seeps into my flesh
and finds its home nestled amongst my bones.
Until the truth always knows the way home.

— Becca Lee

To be who you are
is to be enough.
To share who you are
is to share enough.
To do what you love
is to do enough.

There is no race to win
and nothing to be proven,
only dreams to be nurtured,
a self to be expressed,
and love to be shared.

Never doubt your worth,
and always know,
without any doubt,
that you are truly valued.

— Donna Newman

Strong Women Know Who They Are

Our first job in life as women, I think, is to get to know ourselves. And I think a lot of times we don't do that. We spend our time pleasing, satisfying, looking out into the world to define who we are — listening to the messages, the images, the limited definitions that people have of who we are. And that's true for women of color for sure. There is a limited box that we are put in, and if we live by that limited definition, we miss out on a lot of who we are.

— Michelle Obama

If you know yourself well
and have developed a sense
of confidence in yourself
If you are honest with yourself
and honest with others
If you follow your heart
and adhere to your own truths
you are ready to share yourself
you are ready to set goals
you are ready to find happiness
And the more you love
and the more you give
and the more you feel
the more you will receive
from love
and the more you will receive
from life
　　　　　　— Susan Polis Schutz

Remember, Woman, you were born
life giver, miracle creator, magic maker.
You were born with the heart of a thousand mothers,
open and fearless and sweet.
You were born with the fire of Queens & conquerors,
warrioress blood you bleed.
You were born with the wisdom of sages & shamans,
no wound can you not heal.
You were born the teller of your own tale,
before none should you kneel.

You were born with an immeasurable soul
reaching out past infinity.
You were born to desire with passion, abandon,
and to name your own destiny.
Remember, Woman, remember
you are more than you can see.
Remember, Woman, remember
you are loved endlessly.
Remember, Woman, your power and grace,
the depth of your deep sea heart.
Never forget you are Woman, divine,
as you have been from the start.

— Reese Leyva

Strong Women Are More Than Just a Number

As women, we are often analyzed in a myriad
of different ways to see if we measure up.
We are judged to be too big or too small,
too round, too straight, too tall, too short.
We are compared against numbers
like 36-24-36… in inches, in sizes, and in age —
all things that shouldn't matter.

If we are to be measured as women,
let it be by the things that really count —
the depth of our compassion,
our thirst for knowledge,
and our tremendous grace under fire.
Let the breadth of our integrity
and the width of our honor
be more accurate measures
of who we truly are
rather than the size of our jeans
or the date of our birth.

Because in the end, all the inches and ages
and sizes are just numbers…
and numbers don't tell you anything
about the amazing woman inside!

— Suzy Toronto

i was ten
when i first heard the term
thunder thighs
and i wondered how to become
the type of woman
strong enough
to hold thunder
in her very legs
the type of woman
loud enough
to make thunder
when she walks
a storm bringer
drowning out words that
call attention
to thighs and not souls
that call attention to guys
and enable trolls
i wondered how to get
legs of thunder
and if i could get a
tongue of lightning
to go alongside
if i could really
shake institutions
with each step i took

and make a reputation
from all the foundations
i shook
my body
rapidly
expanding
to take up the space
i was told i could never have
clapping thunder
into the atmosphere
and the faces of those
hellbent on my silence and
fear
hear me and my thighs
they are more powerful
than the men
who name them
they are more beautiful
than the world
that hides them…
and my thighs keep growing
asking for more
they're clapping
and shaking
and making a scene
and bringing a storm
and washing things
clean
                    — Kaitlin Shetler

Pretty women wonder where my secret lies.
I'm not cute or built to suit a fashion model's size
But when I start to tell them,
They think I'm telling lies.
I say,
It's in the reach of my arms,
The span of my hips,
The stride of my step,
The curl of my lips.
I'm a woman
Phenomenally.
Phenomenal woman,
That's me.

— Maya Angelou

I am a woman.
I hold up half of the sky.
I am a woman.
I nourish half of the earth.
I am a woman.
The rainbow touches my shoulders.
The universe encircles my eyes.

— Nancy Wood

What I Weigh

(After the I Weigh Movement)

I weigh the sea
I weigh the storm
I weigh a thousand stories long.
I weigh my mother's fortitude and my father's eyes
I weigh the way they look at me with pride
I weigh strength and fearless and the warrior in me.
I weigh all the pain and trauma that made me see
that I have more galaxies inside me than tragedies.
We all weigh joys and darkness and goodness and sin
you see, we are infinite within this skin we are in.
So when they ask you what you weigh
you don't need to look down at any scale.
Instead, simply tell them the truth,
tell them how you
weigh whole universes
and storms and scars and stories too.

— Nikita Gill

Strong Women Love Themselves

Today I asked my body what she needed,
Which is a big deal
Considering my journey of
Not Really Asking That Much.

I thought she might need more water.
Or protein.
Or greens.
Or yoga.
Or supplements.
Or movement.

But as I stood in the shower
Reflecting on her stretch marks,
Her roundness where I would like flatness,
Her softness where I would like firmness,
All those conditioned wishes
That form a bundle of
Never-Quite-Right-Ness,
She whispered very gently:

Could you just love me like this?

— Hollie Holden

You can't control everything that happens in your life, but you can absolutely control how much love you give yourself. And when you are able to completely love the beautiful, unique woman that you are, you will have the strength to face any hardship.

— Alyssa Rienne

Love is
the only true
freedom.
It lets us
cast off our
false exteriors
and be our
real
selves.

— Susan Polis Schutz

Believe
you are beautiful;
cherish your
uniqueness
and be who you are;
through every hardship,
trust yourself
to overcome.
Be strong
when you can,
cry when you can't;
be wise of the past
and embrace now!

Reach out
when you are safe,
hide when you are not,
laugh often…
and listen carefully.
And never be afraid
to love yourself,
for that is where
all peace… is born.

— Pam Reinke

Strong Women Listen to Their Hearts

As the dawn of each morning
peers into your life,
there lies a path to follow.
Delicate whispers can be heard
if you listen to the sound of your heart
and the voice that speaks within you.
If you listen closely to your soul,
you will become aware of your dreams
that are yet to unfold.
You will discover that there lies within you
a voice of confidence and strength
that will prompt you to seek a journey
and live a dream.

Within the depths of your mind,
the purpose and direction of your life
can be determined by listening intently
to the knowledge that you already possess.
Your heart, mind, and soul
are the foundation
of your success and happiness.

In the still of each passing moment,
may you come to understand that
you are capable of reaching a higher destiny.
When you come to believe
    in all that you are
and all that you can become,
there will be no cause for doubt.

— Leslie Neilson

So many choices
So many voices
People tugging a little
People pulling a little
Who to listen to?
Which way to go?
Everyone means well
The sounds are thunderous
The ideas are divergent
The only voice
that must matter
is the one that
resonates in your own heart
The only choice
that must matter
is the one that
you decide is right for you
Only you can decide what
the fabric of your life will be

— Susan Polis Schutz

Go where the heart
longs to go
Don't pay attention to the feet
that want to stay rooted

Go where the mind
wants to explore
Don't worry about the hands
that still want to hold on

Go where your gut
is fearful to go
Don't let your body
sit in one place

Go where your heart
knows it should go

— Natasha Josefowitz

Strong Women
Support One Another

It's so easy for women
    to slip into self-doubt
        and feeling inadequate.
After all,
we shoulder a lot of responsibilities —
    being supportive of our mates,
    nurturing our children,
    staying in touch with extended family,
    holding down jobs
    while holding down the fort at home.

No wonder we sometimes feel
    anxious, exhausted, and insecure.

We need to know
    we're not alone.
We need to hear
    that other women
    share our experiences.
We need reassurance
    that there's someone who understands —
someone who's been there, done that.

As women, we take turns
    encouraging, supporting,
        and cheering one another on.

                — BJ Gallagher

Our power is greatly expanded when we support one another, both at work and in our personal lives. As one of us faces a seemingly impossible challenge or achieves some new goal or struggles with the process of discovery, we all benefit. By sharing our experiences with each other, we get stronger both individually and as a group, and we pave the way for those who will come after us.

— Helene Lerner-Robbins

What do we live for, if it is not to make life less difficult for each other?

— George Eliot
(Mary Anne Evans)

To help one another is part of the religion of our sisterhood.

— Louisa May Alcott

Strong Women
Are Stronger Together

We who inherit the earth
who cheer the new moon peaking
    through the sky
who admire the green leaves of summer
    turning to lustrous reds and yellows
who watch them fall to the ground
    cold, brown and stiff...

We who give birth to new life
    who are exhilarated by the sun rising
    who are romanced by the sun setting
    who dream to the floating clouds...

We who have a passing mark
   on the future of the world
   must have the same heart
   must have compassion for one another
   must have respect for one another
   must understand that though
      we have differences
   we all want the same things
Nothing should divide us

— Susan Polis Schutz

Any woman who sews
or knits or weaves,
who blends colors in a tapestry
or creates a patchwork quilt,
knows by the feel
that a single thread is weak,
but the weaving,
the blending,
the intertwining
with many others
make it strong.

Any woman alone —
without friends
to sustain her,
to nurture and support her,
to hold her with loving arms —
like a single thread, is weak.
But the weaving,
the loving,
the nurturing of others,
the networks of friendship
make her strong.

— Author Unknown

Borrow strength from others — those "warriors" who have already fought and won the battles you are struggling with today. Rejoice in their victories; they are with you in spirit. Draw strength from those who are with you in the battle today, for none of us truly walk alone.

— Nancye Sims

There is nothing more grounding or more empowering than sisterhood. It is pride in knowing we come from a lineage of dreamers, makers, and survivors. It is perseverance in carrying on their legacy by sharing our compassion and understanding, our will and wisdom. It is the comfort in knowing we stand together, in heart and spirit, always.

— Elspeth Jeanne

Won't You Be My Sister?

Mark me a ripple,
Make me a piercing drop
Of froth at the lip of a wave,
Just so I can be but a note
In the roar of this cresting ocean.

Name me breath,
Know me as air
Dancing nude in the tree tops,
Just so I can be but a sigh
In the cry of this changing wind.

Call me heat,
Claim me red
Of flash writhing in fervor
Just so I can be but a spark
In the pulse of a newborn flame.

Hear me as woman,
Have me as your sister
On purpled battlefield breaking day,
So I might say our victory is just beginning.

That you and I are women
No longer trying to woo men
Holding the truth to be self-evident
That all genders are created equal.

See me as change,
Say I am movement,
That I am the year
And I am the era
Of the women.

— Amanda Gorman

Strong Women Are Dreamers

Lean against a tree
and dream your world of dreams
Work hard at what you like to do
and try to overcome all obstacles
Laugh at your mistakes
and praise yourself for learning from them
Pick some flowers
and appreciate the beauty of nature
Be honest with people
and enjoy the good in them

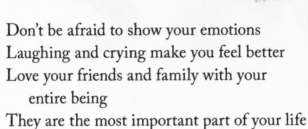

Don't be afraid to show your emotions
Laughing and crying make you feel better
Love your friends and family with your
    entire being
They are the most important part of your life
Feel the calmness on a quiet sunny day
and plan what you want to accomplish in life
Find a rainbow
and live your
world of dreams

— Susan Polis Schutz

Let nothing hold you back from
exploring your wildest fantasies,
wishes, and aspirations.
Don't be afraid to dream big
and to follow your dreams
wherever they may lead you.
Open your eyes to their beauty;
open your mind to their magic;
open your heart to their
possibilities.

Whether your dreams are in color
or in black and white,
whether they are big or small,
easily attainable or almost impossible,
look to your dreams
and make them become reality.
Wishes and hopes are nothing
until you take the first step
toward making them something!
Only by dreaming
will you ever discover
who you are, what you want,
and what you can do.

— Julie Anne Ford

Strong Women Need Rest Too

We push, we strive,
we hurry, we worry,
we reach for the stars,
we plot and plan.
Our days are filled with going and doing,
with wanting more and hoping for better,
with yearning and imagining
how life will be, could be, should be.

But how lovely it is to stop, rest,
and savor the simple pleasures —
to want and enjoy what we already have.
There is no striving, just allowing.
There is no searching, just sweet repose.
As we gather small moments
and small delights
and arrange them to enrich our days,
the spirit and the soul
are nurtured to full blooming.

— Pattie Jansen

Relax… and let everything else
fall into place.
Take one moment for you alone.
Let the day's trials roll off
your shoulders.
Fill your head with thoughts
of nothing at all.
And in that moment —
those brief few seconds where
nothing matters —
breathe deeply and embrace the silence.
Truly relax, and when you wake
to tackle life again,
remember this moment
and let it fill you with courage
and serenity.

— Deana Marino

If the mountain seems too big today
then climb a hill instead.
If the morning brings you sadness
it's okay to stay in bed.
If the day ahead weighs heavy
and your plans feel like a curse,
there's no shame in rearranging,
don't make yourself feel worse.
If a shower stings like needles
and a bath feels like you'll drown,
if you haven't washed your hair for days,
don't throw away your crown.

A day is not a lifetime
a rest is not defeat,
don't think of it as failure,
just a quiet, kind retreat.
It's okay to take a moment
from an anxious, fractured mind,
the world will not stop turning
while you get realigned.
The mountain will still be there
when you want to try again,
you can climb it in your own time,
just love yourself til then.

— Laura Ding-Edwards

Strong Women Aren't Perfect... and That's Okay

Sometimes you
think that you
need to be perfect
that you cannot
make mistakes
At these times
you put so much
pressure on yourself
Try to realize
that you are
like everyone else —
capable of
reaching great potential
but not capable of
being perfect
Just do your best
and realize that
this is enough

— Susan Polis Schutz

It's impossible to be perfect all the time, and it's okay to make mistakes — they're part of what helps you learn, and they make you who you are.

— Ashley Rice

You don't have to be unblemished
    to be beautiful.
You don't have to be unbroken
    to be whole.
You don't have to be unflappable
    to be strong.

These are not flaws; they are foundations
    that form the very heart of your
        beauty, wholeness, and strength.

— Ali Sawyer

for many years I have had
a one-winged glass angel
a small ornament with a string
so I can hang her wherever I please

and it has pleased me to do so
moving her to many different places
depending on my mood and where
I have chosen for the moment to settle

I could, of course, discard her
since she would no longer be able to fly
(not that she ever could, of course)
but still

she reminds me to love my imperfections and
recognize the ways I can still be a blessing
no matter my wounds and limitations

for a long time now she has watched over me
and observed me at my work and play
devoted it seems only to my well-being
serving me wholeheartedly
even in her lopsided presence

and who is to say that she is not
whole and complete just exactly the way she is
a perfect companion for my always whole
and always imperfectly perfect
Self

— Minx Boren

Strong Women Never Give Up

Strong women are those who know the road ahead will be strewn with obstacles, but they still choose to walk it because it's the right one for them.

Strong women are those who make mistakes, who admit to them, learn from those failures, and then use that knowledge.

Strong women are easily hurt, but they still extend their hearts and hands, knowing the risk and accepting the pain when it comes.

Strong women are sometimes beat down by life, but they still stand back up and step forward again.

Strong women are afraid. They face fear and move ahead to the future, as uncertain as it can be.

Strong women are not those who succeed the first time. They're the ones who fail time and again, but still keep trying until they succeed.

Strong women face the daily trials of life, sometimes with a tear, but always with their heads held high as the new day dawns.

— Brenda Hager

Sometimes you will fight your way
through battle after battle
and show your strength and courage
by being a *warrior.*
Sometimes you will wait, listen to your heart,
find wisdom to take the right path,
and show your strength and courage
by being *patient.*
Sometimes you will stand up
for what you believe in,
say "no" to that which is not
compatible with your values,
and show your strength and courage
by being *true to yourself.*

Sometimes you will open new doors for yourself
even when you seem too tired to go on.
You will find the energy to see a new dawn —
a new point of view — and create a new
direction where none seems possible.
You will show your strength and courage
by being *optimistic...*
But no matter how many times
you are knocked down,
with strength and courage
you will always rise again.

— Bonnie St. John

Imagine a Woman

Imagine a woman who believes it is right and good she is a woman. A woman who honors her experience and tells her stories. Who refuses to carry the sins of others within her body and life.

Imagine a woman who trusts and respects herself. A woman who listens to her needs and desires. Who meets them with tenderness and grace.

Imagine a woman who acknowledges the past's influence on the present. A woman who has walked through her past. Who has healed into the present.

Imagine a woman who authors her own life. A woman who exerts, initiates, and moves on her own behalf. Who refuses to surrender except to her truest self and wisest voice.

Imagine a woman who names her own gods. A woman who imagines the divine in her image and likeness. Who designs a personal spirituality to inform her daily life.

Imagine a woman in love with her own body.
A woman who believes her body is enough, just
as it is. Who celebrates its rhythms and cycles as
an exquisite resource.

Imagine a woman who honors the body of the
Goddess in her changing body. A woman who
celebrates the accumulation of her years and
her wisdom. Who refuses to use her life-energy
disguising the changes in her body and life.

Imagine a woman who values the women in
her life. A woman who sits in circles of women.
Who is reminded of the truth about herself
when she forgets.

Imagine yourself as this woman.

— Patricia Lynn Reilly

Strong Women Can Change the World

There are women who make things better... simply by showing up. There are women who make things happen. There are women who make their way. There are women who make a difference. And women who make us smile. There are women who do not make excuses. Women who cannot be replaced. There are women of wit and wisdom who — through strength and courage — make it through. There are women who change the world every day... women like you.

— Ashley Rice

There's no mountain
you can't climb;
no storm you can't weather.
You have the power of
the universe on your side.
You were made to soar.

— Linda E. Knight

The seed of greatness
lies within you.
Nurture it, and there
will be nothing you can't do.

— Lisa Marie Yost

You Are an Incredible, Strong Woman

You are such a strong woman,
and you have wisdom and insight
well beyond what you give yourself
    credit for.
If you don't believe me,
just take a quick look back at
    the roads you've traveled
and at all the pitfalls, troubles,
and difficult times
you have already passed through
    and risen above.

You are a survivor
and a wonderful woman full of
    spirit and energy.

— Linda Hersey

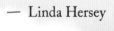

Each year you grow stronger
and more confident
in who you are,
setting new goals and
challenging yourself
for the year to come.

Today and every day,
remember all the things
you have to offer and
all the beauty you encompass
within your magnificent character.
You are rich in talent and ambition,
shining in every endeavor
you embark upon.
You extend your generosity
and kindness to everyone you encounter,
spreading such positive energy
through your gentle actions.

All of this has created
the amazing woman you have always been
and will continue to be.

— Jeanmarie A. Swiontkowski

Acknowledgments

We gratefully acknowledge the permission granted by the following authors, publishers, and authors' representatives to reprint poems or excerpts in this publication:

Barbara J. Hall for "The way you see yourself...." Copyright © 2022 by Barbara J. Hall. All rights reserved.

Random House, an imprint and division of Penguin Random House LLC, for "We don't have to do..." from A WOMAN'S WORTH by Marianne Williamson. Copyright © 1993 by Marianne Williamson. And for "Pretty women wonder..." from AND STILL I RISE: A BOOK OF POEMS by Maya Angelou. Copyright © 1978 by Maya Angelou. All rights reserved.

Becca Lee (@beccaleepoetry) for "And I will keep reminding myself...," Instagram image, January 12, 2021, https://www.instagram.com/p/CJ8SKuFLg_m/. Copyright © 2021 by Becca Lee. All rights reserved.

Reese Leyva for "Remember, Woman, you were born..." from reeseleyva.com, https://reeseleyva.com/2015/04/04/remember-woman/. Copyright © 2015 by Reese Leyva. All rights reserved.

Suzy Toronto for "As women, we are often analyzed...." Copyright © 2014 by Suzy Toronto. All rights reserved.

Kaitlin Shetler (@kaitlinshetler) for "i was ten...," Instagram post, August 25, 2021, https://www.instagram.com/p/CTAKS5AsWdB/. Copyright © 2021 by Kaitlin Shetler. All rights reserved.

Nancy Wood Literary Trust for "I am a woman..." from MANY WINTERS by Nancy C. Wood. Copyright © 1974 by Nancy C. Wood. For more poems by Nancy Wood, visit www.nancywood.com. All rights reserved.

David Higham Associates for "What I Weigh" by Nikita Gill (@nikita_gill) Instagram image, August 17, 2018, https://www.instagram.com/p/Bmln65aHL9g/. Copyright © 2018 by Nikita Gill. All rights reserved.

Hollie Holden (@hollieholdenlove) for "Today I asked my body...," Instagram image, April 17, 2018, https://www.instagram.com/p/Bhr4l03AEfl/. Copyright © 2018 by Hollie Holden. All rights reserved.

Pam Reinke for "Believe you are beautiful...." Copyright © 2006 by Pam Reinke. All rights reserved.

Natasha Josefowitz for "Go where the heart..." from TOO WISE TO WANT TO BE YOUNG AGAIN. Copyright © 1996 by Natasha Josefowitz. All rights reserved.

BJ Gallagher for "It's so easy for women...." Copyright © 2007 by BJ Gallagher. All rights reserved.

Helene Lerner-Robbins for "Our power is greatly..." from OUR POWER AS WOMEN. Copyright © 1996 by Helene Lerner-Robbins. All rights reserved.

Amanda Gorman (@amandascgorman) for "Won't You Be My Sister?", Instagram image, December 29, 2018, https://www.instagram.com/p/Br_FZtiAGoq/. Copyright © 2018 by Amanda Gorman. All rights reserved.

Pattie Jansen for "We push, we strive...." Copyright © 2017 by Pattie Jansen. All rights reserved.

Laura Ding-Edwards for "If the mountain seems..." from THE MOUNTAIN. Copyright © 2019 by Laura Ding-Edwards. All rights reserved.

Minx Boren for "for many years I have had...." Copyright © 2017 by Minx Boren. All rights reserved.

Patricia Lynn Reilly for "Imagine a Woman" from A GOD WHO LOOKS LIKE ME. Copyright © 1995 by Patricia Lynn Reilly. All rights reserved.

Linda E. Knight for "There's no mountain...." Copyright © 2022 by Linda E. Knight. All rights reserved.

A careful effort has been made to trace the ownership of selections used in this anthology in order to obtain permission to reprint copyrighted material and give proper credit to the copyright owners. If any error or omission has occurred, it is completely inadvertent, and we would like to make corrections in future editions provided that written notification is made to the publisher:

BLUE MOUNTAIN ARTS, INC., P.O. Box 4549, Boulder, Colorado 80306.